On A Cold, Windy Hill
Essays

Sharon Slaton Howell

Black Wolf Press
2018

Printed in the USA

Published by:
    Black Wolf Press
    1800 Grand Avenue
    Knoxville, Tennessee 37916

Printed and bound in the United States of America.

4th Printing

Library of Congress Control Number: 2017945451

Table of Contents

Born to Write?

Perhaps so. I write because I can't *not* write.
Life is so much more alive when I'm writing. Was
I born to do this? Probably. I recall something
the Editor of The Christian Science Monitor
said to me once. After we returned from living
in Southeast Asia, we moved to Boston and I got
a job with the newspaper. I had begun writing
seriously a couple of years before, had had some
articles published in magazines and the Monitor.
Of course, I wanted to do much more. He said
something I won't forget: "Anyone can be a writer-
-that is, if he or she is born wanting to."

Whether or not this holds true for everyone,
I can't say. But those fortunate people who would
rather put words on paper or a computer than just
about anything else have it in them to succeed, I
do believe. They will not be stopped from getting
their thoughts and ideas and insights out there.

Burning desire always finds a way. My experience has been that the one who *must* write is going to do it--no matter what, despite upheaval in his or her life, not feeling physically up to it at times, whatever. And rejection after rejection doesn't stop the true writer. And there's plenty of that to go around. I love what Winston Churchill once said, or wrote: "Success consists in going from failure to failure without loss of enthusiasm."

And on rejection, I once took every "We regret to say…" letter I got personally. I was sure the Editor didn't like me! Of course, he or she didn't know me in most cases. If we personalize every "no" and get down about it, our writing could be permanently sidelined. It could be that a particular piece just isn't what an Editor is looking for, or feels the audience their publication reaches won't be interested in what we've submitted. When I was first sending poems out to New England magazines, one poem happened to mention walking late at night with a big black dog. Well, would you believe that Editor loved the poem, which I feel to this day was because she had a big black dog she loved to walk at night. Such is the way things can go. Naturally, being early in my career, I was up in the clouds for days at appearing alongside some very accomplished poets. Almost everything I sent this woman thereafter got me that dreaded letter.

I feel that writers have so little say in whether they write or not. Thoughts begin to flow, words are set to go, and inspiration must be attended to, with singleness of heart. Those who do this gathering of ideas from above, from heights divine if this is what you believe, or least from someplace outside of themselves, inhabit a universe they're in--but all too often not of. So, speaking for myself, I give others involved in the creative act of writing consideration kind. I think our world is richer by far that writers are as they are. Words are so magical, potent, long-lasting. Is there anything words cannot do?

Having received so much encouragement along the way, I always go out of mine to give a few kind words to others who aspire to write. I'm no stranger to discouragement, was nearly shut down several years ago by an Editor who took over a magazine I had been published in for some time. This former ad man from Australia decided one day he didn't like the way I wrote. There were a couple of my manuscripts in the department awaiting publication and he said on the phone one day, "I don't intend to publish these." I was devastated, almost panicky. "What outlet will I have now for my writing?" I worried. He had to be the meanest man that ever walked down a city street. I stopped writing for awhile--a miserable time for me.

But eventually I started up again. And by this time, the Editor in question had moved on and the new man actually thought my articles had something to say to the public. So, remembering how it feels to not get any encouragement, then to have kind souls cross my path who took the time to say, "I like the way you express your thoughts. I've gotten a lot out of your poem or essay. Keep at it", I don't pass up an opportunity to help others when I see creativity struggling to get out.

Who can estimate the good we can do when we take a little time out to notice what others are about, to show some appreciation, to offer some encouragement. A life can be turned around, inspired thought unsealed, latent talent revealed, with a few kind words.

From time to time I run across someone who is obviously alive to life, a sensitive soul who feels things deeply. I ask them, "Do you write, or paint, or do something else of a creative nature?" And just the other day, I put this question to a very nice young man who serves me at a favorite restaurant. His face brightened and he said, "Oh, I'd love to write! There's so much I want to say. But I don't know how to get started." To which I replied, "You've got to get the words down on paper. Or a computer. Then you'll have something to work with. I'm sure you have something to share with the world." I left thinking that this man was encouraged to try since someone took the time to listen to him and show a little interest.

So, you never know, this aspiring writer may just end up writing a book someday--all because of a few kind words.

A friend from Melbourne, Australia is one of these individuals I owe a debt of gratitude to for his encouragement. Paul was an accomplished poet and sculptor, and always took the time to comment on whatever I sent him. We didn't agree sometimes on the way I chose to express myself. But his keen eye was always welcome. He has passed on now, but I feel he's still writing, sustained by that unseen, *felt* Presence so many writers know. Whatever they may call it.

I run across people who will tell me, I so want to be a writer, but how do you know what to write? I always want to say, just look around you. There are so many potential topics. To me, Nature presents endless inspiration for an aspiring author. There is no dearth of possibilities for artistic expression and fulfillment for those with eyes to see--infinite themes to lose one's self in. Take trees, for just one example. One could capture the way light plays on trunks of trees, or their subtle colors of brown. Then there are rocks, and the many shades of patterns of moss and lichen clinging on them. For the person who yearns to express himself in poetry or prose, Nature provides such a gift. Personally, I cannot look at earth's loveliness, and feeling bedazzled, not want others to view the incredible beauty with some of the intensity that I do.

Of course, it may not be Nature that turns a person on. It might be animals, his or her pets, which one could write about and not run dry for a long time. It might be colorful people one knows or observes in his daily rounds. It could be a desire to tackle philosophical or religious topics. But whatever engages one's thought, there are potential readers who may well find what one has to say worth reading, even rewarding, or life-changing.

When someone I'm trying to buck up is still hesitant about putting thoughts on paper, who doesn't have the confidence to get under way, I tell them, what you have to share is as valid as anyone else's. So have your say. If it's in your heart, I have found over many years that it is going to reach the hearts of others.

Speaking for myself, when engaged in a work of a literary persuasion, sometimes creations show up at my mental door fully clothed. At others times, at the completion of what I can only call one of those rascals, I feel I've run a marathon. Or tried to. But however writing comes--easy, or labored--like it was for Flaubert (so they say) who took all one morning to put a comma in, and all afternoon to take it out, there are few things in my book that can compare to a piece of writing that is "there". When words have established themselves, and there's no more to be shared on a particular subject, insight, or conviction--at least at the time. What a feeling this is. And an added joy is knowing that people in parts of the world I'll never probably see will be reading what I've written. When it comes to writing, life doesn't need to be any better than this!

Writing, whether books or on-line, can be so rewarding. In 2008, I began a blog "For Love of Christ Jesus and Christian Science" and it continues today. Prior to starting my own blog, I had contributed many poems and essays to various sites on-line. I met several lovely writers from distant places along the way.

Of course, whether one's books are in bookstores, or his or her writing is out there in cyberspace, there is the smut factor to be considered for some of us. A lot of trash is found in both venues. I asked myself before starting my blog, "Do I want my certainly clean, rather lofty thoughts to be mixed in with so much, let me just say it, pornographic material?" But I decided the good that could be done outweighed the bad of being on-line. Readers from many parts of the world have thanked me for this or that posting, telling me how helpful a given piece meant to them. So it turned out to be the right step for me.

And awhile back, interestingly enough, my blog led an Editor of The New York Times to contact me with a request to do a short essay for them on health care for children. I'm sure it was the information in my profile, listing the hundreds of pieces published over the years in magazines and newspapers, as well as my 7 books at that time in public and university libraries all the globe that got me invited to contribute. In addition, the over 30 national libraries of the world that have added one or more of my books to their permanent collections.

Bottom line, who knows how far-reaching our writing may be? Opportunities for expressing one's inspiration and joy in life are endless, are they not?

Ah, Autumn

My favorite season of them all. How do I enjoy September, October, and November? By:

***decorating our front porch with chrysanthemums, usually in shades of yellow and gold and rust, sometimes wine. Of course, I have to add just the right pumpkins. I check them out carefully at the roadside stands as though they're going to be permanent, so important is it to get just the right shape and size. And with a stem that curls just so and has a touch of green on it. After fall is over, and Christmas decorations start going up, I move pumpkins around to my garden bench where squirrels can get at them if they wish. I put out Cletus, our harvest figure. He's the cutest little fellow, about 3 feet high, with a farmer's cover-alls, plaid shirt, straw hat, and happy expression on his face. When I found him at Wal-Mart some years ago, just knew he was the one I had to take home. I asked a dear friend who lives here in Tennessee, "What's a good Southern name for a farmer?" Betty thought for awhile, and came back with Cletus.

***taking a drive through the countryside, exploring back roads, to see pumpkins in mist--so very picturesque, pure poetry to me.

***eating crisp apples and cinnamon donuts. I've even added yummy hot chocolate with lots of whipped cream over at Starbucks, imbibed outside early on chilly mornings. My favorite spot is a table at one corner of the building where the cold winds come whipping around.

***reveling in autumn leaves. I make angels in the leaves on our neighbor's hill (yes, I do this); standing outside when leaves are pelting down just like I'm standing under a rain shower, delighting as they land in my hair; rolling in a pile of just-raked leaves with one of our dogs who gets a kick out of messing everything up.

***sleeping with the windows open. (Is there anything quite like non-air conditioned air?)

***Another of my autumn joys is cold, crisp enough nights to burrow under a puffy comforter. Never had one of these, of course, growing up in Texas. And might not have here in Tennessee except for a magazine article I subscribed to. I happened to see one issue with the focus on up-state New York during autumn. In lovely photographs, charming inns were featured where tourists and visitors to see the foliage could spend a comfortable night or two. Colorful, inviting comforters adorned the beds. Suddenly, I wanted one of these, and I found just the right one.

***taking the time to watch October's mellow golden sun stream through wind-rippled branches and perform a ballet across rug, bookcase, and wall--one of Nature's many magic shows.

***in order to have our yard light up come spring, planting dozens of daffodils, putting in pretty-faced pansies.

You fellow autumn-aficionados no doubt have your own rituals for celebrating the season, but these are some of mine.

Asian Adventure

It didn't seem so at the time, but living in Seoul, Korea for over a year while my husband was completing his military commitment turned out to be an experience I wouldn't have missed for anything.

Was I scared at first? Never having been away from home very far, much less to a foreign country to live there, I certainly was. But we hadn't been married for long, and I so wanted to join my husband. What relief it was when someone from the headquarters of my church asked if I would be interested in becoming Minister for Armed Services Personnel in Southeast Asia during that time. I would be based in Seoul. I accepted and made plans to fly on my own to Korea. Of course, the Army didn't pay the fare. We did, with parents' help. But it was worth it.

A few weeks after John arrived at his new post, I took off on my adventure, first to San Francisco, then to Anchorage, Alaska, then on to Asia. Tell me landing in such a foreign environment was not both frightening and exciting. I was worried that my husband wouldn't get away from up north near the DMZ (demilitarized zone as it is known). "How will I get a cab and get out to the suburbs where John had rented a teeny apartment for me, and for us, when he could get away", I wondered. But there he was in the crowd! Never will I forget my relief and joy at seeing his face.

Strange to say, I wanted some American food, a hamburger or something. We stopped at a local restaurant and managed to convey to the waitress what we wanted. It didn't much resemble a hamburger, but they tried. This was the first of what would be brand-new culinary experiences, in Seoul, and later when we traveled to Japan and Hong Kong.

For a wife or dependents to be in the country at that time was considered a hardship tour. For good reason. It was certainly this for me. Roughing it was one way to put our living conditions. And I was lonely much of the time, but did have my church work and attendance downtown at the local Society. Koreans are resilient people, so admirable and tough. And we didn't have heat in the church, so had to wear our coats in the cold months. And so Spartan were the inhabitants' lives that when we put a soda pop can outside our door to be picked up or a copy of a US newspaper my husband had sent to Seoul, we would hear the patter of feet and like magic, whatever had been discarded was whisked away and made use of. Often in an imaginative way. Nothing went to waste in that place.

To fill up the time, and have some extra income, I was secretary to an American professor doing research for the Department of Defense. When I got home to our one-room apartment I would sit on what was our bed--a futon mattress--and write articles for The Christian Science Monitor. I had started doing this at that cheap, rented dining table in Maryland where John first was stationed. Having them readily published encouraged me to keep writing, and to branch out a bit, into magazine articles.

Riding on a local bus was quite an experience. To Koreans, we smelled like dairy products--milk, cheese, and butter we learned. And to us, the amazing amount of garlic that goes into their food was nearly overpowering when they breathed on us in a crowded bus. The ladies would giggle, point to my round eyes, fascinated with our different looks.

When John could get away from the post, some Korean friends we had made would show us around and introduce us to unusual (for us) food, take us on trips to the country. We were surprised and delighted that Seoul had four distinct seasons, just like we were used to. And those stunning blue skies when cold winds from Siberia would sweep down and make everything so clean and crisp. I've never seen a sky quite that shade of blue. The scenery, though nothing like we had ever seen at home naturally, was quite beautiful.

Little by little, I grew accustomed to the

new culture and unlike some other wives, chose to stay on, homesick as I was. And midway in John's tour of duty, we visited Japan and Hong Kong. And by the time we were to return to the USA, both of us had come to love the Korean people, had made many friends, and wished we could live in Korea permanently. For years after our return to the States, we tried to think of ways we could live there. We yearned to help the people we loved. But it never worked out for us to move back there. Of course, we went back several times to Korea, and other spots in Southeast Asia. My husband had learned some Japanese, and we toured that country extensively. Also, loved going back to Hong Kong, for a ride on the cable car, for the marvelous Chinese dishes, for the fascinating sights and sounds surrounding us.

Besides opening up new vistas for me personally, what I most gained from my Asian adventure was respect for peoples of different nationalities. I felt such compassion for the way so many had almost nothing in monetary value but were happy and hard-working nonetheless. To get back home and be able to just turn on the faucet and have non-rusty water took some getting used to. And the abundant food Americans had! It revolted us to see so much food just thrown out when people in other parts of the world had too little to eat.

My life would have been much less rich had I not lived and worked in Asia, and for this I will always be thankful that it opened us for me. For us.

If I Could Live Anywhere...

...it would be Scotland. Loved the horizon-broadening aspects of living in Seoul, Korea and Boston, Massachusetts. And now in the South which has proved rewarding in many ways.

But it's Scotland that speaks to me. Curious, isn't it, when this is a place I've never even been to. As a generally happy individual, I'm usually contented with wherever I happen to live. But I would like to live in Scotland someday.

What is it about Scotland I love? I cannot tell you. Is it the many illustrious men and women who have done their country proud? I so admire that "when the tough have had enough, a Scot gets going" mentality. William Wallace, Scotland's national hero, personifies this to me. I was electrified by a documentary we saw. The courage of this single man to stand alone for freedom for his beloved Scotland! There is no mystery why William Wallace is so revered far and wide.

Then there is Andrew Carnegie, whose vast giving to establish public libraries so that the poorest among us could read free, has inspired me greatly. Growing up in Dallas, Texas, my parents were wonderful at giving us all they could afford, but buying books was not in their budget. So this is where I came to love free public libraries. As Carnegie wrote about this: "A library outranks any other one thing a community can do to benefit its people. It is a never failing spring in a desert." The charitable work this philanthropist did, all across the globe. How many men, women, and children have been blessed by his unselfish endeavors.

I have known Scots personally, of course. One stands out--a lovely woman who became employed at a large care facility in Boston, Massachusetts where I was one of the trustees. She had been manager of a hotel in Edinburgh. Observing the gracious, efficient way she conducted her duties at her new post, I couldn't help but be impressed. We were fortunate to have her in charge of things.

A long-time resident of East Tennessee told me that this state was settled largely by Scots. Each year there are Scottish Festivals throughout the state. Those of Scottish ancestry attend in large number, and there special food and exciting games can be enjoyed by all. These events are open to the public. I haven't yet been, but would like to.

Last but certainly not least, it's Scotland's natural beauty that captures me so. Wind-blown grasses, rocky hills, stepping stones in crystal streams, picturesque bridges, stone walls old, castles, ancient oaks dappled in golden light, carpets of brightly-colored leaves in autumn, daffodils gracing churchyard and meadow in the spring.

And yes, even the rain. Perhaps it was growing up in hot, dry ol' Texas, maybe I'm just one of those persons who like being out in the rain. But what I think accounts for my delight with it is the drought year after year we've been through here in the South.

I recall two summers especially when my continuing worry was how are the trees in our woods going to survive this? Blazing sun and not a drop of moisture was taking its toll, not just on them, but on me as well. Then the weather pattern changed, mercifully, and rains finally came. Buckets of life-giving rain. Cracks in the ground closed up, the grass turned green, our creek filled up, and all was happy again.

What fun it is to sit on our garden bench under a canopy of trees listening to the drops hitting the leaves. I love to walk out alone in the rain when the sky turns to night and street lamps come on, the raindrops glistening on dark, green leaves. I splash in puddles just like a kid. Getting wrapped up in a downy comforter with a good book, just listening to rain hit the roof is pure joy. As is going outside after the rain has stopped and looking at the droplets hanging off ends of branches. They look like diamonds to me-- diamonds from the sky.

In short, seeing lightning, hearing thunder, then going to my window and getting to exclaim, "It's raining!"

And speaking of rain, I love storms-- especially being out in them. Not storms that bring destruction to people and property, of course. But to feel nature in its element is a delight. To experience the sensation of wind and rain on my face is something I can't get enough of.

And where I would most like to be when it's storming? In the Orkney Islands. Not that I've ever been there at all either. But it's a place I once saw on television that has excited my imagination and stayed with me.

There was the most quaint, little dwelling, perched not far from the sea (which one, I don't know), probably the North Sea off Scotland's coast. But the photographer had gotten the feel of the raging storm. And I could just imagine us all snug inside the cottage, under a warm blanket, with a mug of strong tea and perhaps a scone or two. And a good book, waiting out the storm. Not that we wouldn't have spent some time walking our dogs along that coast, with the rain and wind pelting us. What pure joy this would be.

The Beauty of Solitude

How one can prefer society's noise to solitude's peace and quiet is more than the true lover of nature can comprehend. At least, I can't. If there's anything I dread, it's being in the company of someone who has nothing to say-- yet goes on and on and never knows when to end. How can such infinite beauty as our heavenly Father spreads before us be adequately appreciated while in a crowd of people.

It's indisputable (at least it is to me), contemplating nature and garrulity are incompatible. On forays in the wild, give me a soulful quiet. And possibly a companion (or two or three of the four-legged and furry kind) who know the value of silence.

I love being out in the woods or a forest when winter is past, when mother Nature gets out her spring dress. How many shades of green there have to be is anybody's guess--whitest tints to yellow, with emerald, olive and dark green, with countless hues in between. The hillsides are decked out and rocks and trees besides, with leaves and lichen, and the softest moss. Taking in spring's glory is enough for me. Who needs to hear chatter at a time like this?

Don't get me wrong. I'm as convivial as the next fellow. There's nothing like being with friends from time to time, sharing a delicious dinner and good conversation. It's just that I don't feel bereft without this. I've never had a restless desire for personal company.

Doesn't always having to have people around us, not willing to be just alone with one's own thoughts, bespeak a lack of inner resources? It seems so to me. And it's possible to be in a roomful of people, and yet feel lonely. Conversely, when we've taken the time, and effort, to develop interests beyond ourselves, we can be all alone humanly speaking, yet not be lonely at all.

Whether it's an interest in great music, or literature, or learning a foreign language, or getting involved in some activity that helps our fellow beings, the right sense of solitude need not be solitary.

A Love for Nature

There isn't. But one might almost think there is some Native American back there in my family somewhere. It's all I can do to not be out of doors most of the time. The four seasons are such a delight to me--each one filled with beautiful things and holding abiding fascination, an endless array of scenes to marvel at and write about.

Whence this penchant for Nature? I don't recall being swayed by it growing up in the Southwest. Perhaps it was too hot down there. No, this isn't it. It seemed to have surfaced at the same time poems began to appear. We were living in scenic New England and one day when I was driving back home from Wellesley, Massachusetts, there was this quaint old stone wall in Weston, stretching for miles. And there planted along it, were glorious daffodils. I had been reading William Wordsworth's poetry, and that scene brought about my first poem to be published in a major American poetry magazine:

Daffodils

April, with its yellow, green and cold

Brings to this England new

Beauty such as Wordsworth saw: O delight!

Daffodils gracing field and pasture,

Daffodils adorning stone walls old.

Gifts of nature fade from mortal view,

But they, like scenes immortal poets

Paint for all eternity,

To mental sight, lovely linger

All year through.

I had thought of trying my hand at poems, but some wise (?!) and published friends discouraged this, saying "I don't think you ought to try poetry; you're not gifted that way." So I didn't try, for too many years. Then one wonderful day unforgettable, poems began to appear--poems which have warmed readers, made them laugh and weep. And in some cases, made them want to amend their lives. Truly.

Nature, which to me is one big poem or essay waiting to be written about, provided so many topics over the years. It is still doing this. So, whether it's winter, spring, summer or fall, she gives anyone plenty to contemplate, to enjoy, to marvel at, in them all.

Living on the Light

It's has been said that writers live on the light of Nature. Whether this is true for all or not, it certainly applies to me. The light of Nature enchants me. The way it paints on skies, trees, rock, flowers.

Take skies, to start at the top. I love looking at clouds after the rain has stopped and the sun comes shining through. Hallelujah-chorus shafts of light stream down. Soft, quiet beauty is all around. And the air, the air smells first-day-of-creation new. It's enough to just be alive at such times. I've noticed that the skies in my state are not quite as vast as the ones I knew in Texas, but they're a close second.

Then there's the sunrises and sunsets, an endless combination of colors only the Creator could come up with. Let me describe for you one morning in particular--peach and rose and gold, cream and baby blue, and rimmed with fire, clouds of slate. It was spectacular. That's the only word that can do it justice. What made this sunrise so riveting to me was the sun behind the dark grey clouds, illuminating them. I was driving along, late for an appointment, but had to pull over by the side of the road to just ooh and ahh. There have been many others, of course. But this one stands out as something only a master painter could put on canvas.

Light is seen in so many lovely ways: in ducks gliding across a pond, leaving long streaks of shining in their wake. In the happy eyes of a little child. In any face that is aglow with love. Speaking of which, I've seen men and women whom the world would not describe as beautiful, yet were because of the love for someone or some thing which lit up their countenance.

Then there's what I call dancing light. During the golden month of October, when the sun is setting, the loveliest patterns show up on kitchen walls and our family room where we spend much time. It's as though light is performing a ballet. I could watch what light does for hours on end.

And not to overlook late at night when the light of the moon makes the landscape magical. This is certainly a wonderful time to spend out of the house. When there's a huge moon, one can almost read by its glow. And to get to walk our dogs at such a time is especially rewarding. One evening I recall that one of our dogs needed to go out around 2:30 am. We ended up walking down several back streets, just enjoying the peace and beauty. It was so still, perfectly lovely out.

And stars. I love December days, when it's nearly dark and it's time to go out in twilight's chill, down our long street to the cul-de-sac and back. Deepest-blue sky soon turns to black. The solitude is glorious, companioned only by serene, bright host overhead, and big black dog underfoot.

Many places may have these, but in June for about a week Nature puts on quite a show that people travel to the Great Smoky Mountains nearby to view: thousands upon thousands of fireflies, trees and bushes flashing with tiny, white lights. A sight, this synchronous firefly display.

Can't you see how light in its myriad manifestations can inspire creativity--whether in artist or writer?

On a Cold, Windy Hill

We come down from the hiking trails through our favorite forest, our big black dog and I. We pause, always. I love this spot, especially when the winds are whipping around on cold days, as it is today. It's late October, the most glorious month in the year for me. The sky is a beautiful blue, with puffy white clouds here and there. There may be a hint of blustery weather coming. We have often stood out on our hill on such days, loving every minute of it.

Whence this joy in cold, windy days? Perhaps it is this way for you, but sometimes we see images that stay with us long after. Several years ago, I happened to see a vast meadow of purple, pink, and white wildflowers in a Nature program. It was somewhere on the Oregon coast. Stunning scene. Not a word was spoken, just the sound of the wind, blowing the flowers more beautiful.

Then, a documentary on wolf packs at Jackson Hole, Wyoming completely captured my imagination. It was Christmas, and it was pure magic. Trees laden with ice, the snowflakes glistening in the moonlight, wolves running through the deep snow so amazingly fast and free. I sat there on our sofa with tears running down my face. Hard to explain to you such a reaction, but there it was. I couldn't help rejoicing that God had made such wonderful creatures.

Later, I saw another program highlighting wolves. A scene that never has left me was one black wolf, standing on a hilltop in what was obviously cold weather, the sound of the wind all around. I could feel myself on that hilltop with this magnificent animal, just drinking in the cold, windy outdoors, wherever it was. Probably somewhere out West.

We have a small hill in our front yard where one of our dogs and I sit out on cold, windy days. The winds come around the corner of the house, rippling the grass, enveloping dog and me.

This seems strange to some people, I know. Case in point: one day a neighbor from the down the street, an Indian lady, happened to walk by during of these sessions. She came up to us, alarmed. "Are you all right?" she asked with concern. I saw you sitting in the grass and thought you might need help." "We're fine" I told her. "We often do this. We enjoy being outdoors on days like this."

Some people find wind foreboding, rather scary in some way. They would rather not be out on windy days. As for me, I always feel protected, safe when winds blow, even on stormy days if such do not get out of hand and cause harm. Often I just stand outside and lift my arms to the sky, in a child's delight at the glories of Nature. I *feel* God's presence all around.

What is wind without trees? Wind makes trees more enchanting to me. They seem even more alive, in a way. Trees have got to be one God's greatest gifts. Anyway I choose to look at one of these--standing, sitting up, lying down, I never tire of gazing at trees. Sometimes when outside on our lawn with one of our dogs, I actually lie down and look up at trees. In this position, they seem especially majestic.

Desert landscapes no doubt possess a certain kind of beauty. But for me, all that starkness with no trees in sight would do me in. I have to be surrounded by trees--love them, cannot imagine living where there weren't lost of them around. And large ones at that.

You've heard of people who describe themselves as tree-huggers. Well, I am one. And then some. I have actually put my arms around them. Or tried to with the big ones. Trees seem almost alive, in a greater sense than just being living things. I can imagine them talking to each other on those evenings when all is quiet and world is asleep. And the sounds that wind makes blowing through them. I love it.

There's a place we visit in a local park and as we make the winding climb up 3 levels of the woods, I see a clearing that I've named my cathedral of the trees. While I've had my share of uplifted, holy moments while sitting in a church made of stone, I do believe that on a bench at the edge of a lovely forest, I'm quite near the Divine. I often sit there in reflection, all alone--except for the One who created that beauty.

And even tree trunks have their interest. We saw one on a trek through the forest that was full of charm. This one took home the prize. About 3 feet high, bright green moss growing here and there, English ivy up one side, the cutest toadstool at its base. I could picture tiny creatures abiding in its weather-sculpted crevices. You've got personality, kid, I said to myself.

Then there are the glories of autumn trees. I could write page after page on the show they put on for us. In September our woods are what I call all green and light, the sunlight softening everything, a few colored leaves making their debut. Then October, all golden and light, trees with leaves of red, yellow, orange and wine, in stunning variation/combination. Even in early November, Nature's fall palette of brightly-colored leaves is still on display.

If you haven't done so, consider a trip to New England in the fall, just to see the spectacular foliage. I once thought when I saw Nature calendars showing autumn leaves that the reds were touched up. Not so. When we visited Vermont, the colors, particularly those reds, were nothing short of dazzling.

The American poet, Joyce Kilmer, had it right in my view when he wrote: "Only God can make a tree." And windy, cold hills I might add.

The Woodland Creatures
of Willow Gate Rise

We loved those woodland creatures of
Willow Gate Rise that would come around mainly
at night. (Being a poet, I loved the name of our
street, though there wasn't a willow tree or gate
in sight, and only a slight rise in our long road.
The person who chose the name must have been a
writer. But no matter.)

Those animals, especially the raccoons, were
so dear. And for many a year, my husband would
put food out--even after hefty New England
snows and a terrific lot of shoveling to clear their
dinner area. Up to the retaining wall they would
come, settle down on their bottoms, and feast on
the loot. Oh they were so cute! And when baby
raccoons came along, a mother would be quite
tame. With the need to feed so many mouths, she
would seem half starved herself, willing to come up
close to us.

Then one day the moving van came. With a pang we had to leave them behind. Would the new owners follow our instructions and keep those darling things alive? Vain hope, I would think. The couple who bought our house didn't seem to be the animal lovers we were.

We've often wondered how the woodland creatures got along with us gone. But we tried to realize that their Maker would no doubt find a way to sustain them. Perhaps they would go back to the wild (what there was left, what with ever-increasing housing developments springing up), as they had been doing before we welcomed them into our yard.

We had heard somewhere that we shouldn't be feeding wildlife. But John was such a bird lover and put out seed for over 15 species of birds. It became necessary to put something out for wildlife so they wouldn't scarf the birds' food. That was how it all started, and we weren't a bit sorry.

I'm happy to report that the joy of seeing

these little woodland creatures--foxes, possums, skunks, rabbits, chipmunks too--continues to this day in our new home in Tennessee. And every now and then, as it's getting dark, we get to see a cute little raccoon face. And some even come up very close, settle down, and begin to feast.

For several nights now well before dark, a raccoon will come for supper. She may be a mother, and quite hungry earlier in the evening now. Our two dogs are something to watch. They stand on our elevated screened-in porch and watch her eat. Normally, they will bark at just about anything that moves. But they don't. They stand so still, hardly move a muscle and do this for the longest time. We don't know what is so gripping about seeing an animal eat, but it's something they love to do.

A man who does so many repairs around our property built the animals the cutest little house. It's a raised wooden platform, open on all sides where they can get in during bad weather and have dry food. David, master carpenter that he is who never does a job halfway, even added a slanted, shingled roof on their shelter. And he suggested piling some bales of hay under our porch, opening up an opening so they can climb in and sleep and be safe, if any are so inclined. And a possum or possums certainly have availed themselves of this "hotel."

And speaking of possums, there was an incident involving one several years ago we wouldn't want to deal with again. We began to notice a pungent aroma, even in the front yard, and especially as we rounded the corner toward the back yard. Finally, my husband said we needed to find out where this apparently expired animal was coming from. It was clear one of us needed to undertake this chore. And being that wives are sometimes more resilient in such matters, I was elected to do it. Tracing the smell to the hay pile under the porch one early morning, I got long rubber gloves and went to work. I reached into the opening, fished around a bit, went way back to the back and there pressed on what was, or had been, a furry creature. Holding my nose, I proceeded to dig him or her out. We have a woodpile at the back of the woods, and it was there this little thing was deposited under a lot of leaves. Sad for us, but this happens with wildlife.

And just this afternoon, I happened to look out at the birds flitting around at the feeders and what looked back at me through the screen door was a pretty face. It was a raccoon. It was only five o'clock, too early for us to have put the dog food out they eat. Normally, they come around after dark. But this little thing had climbed up the wooden steps to the elevated porch and was looking at me from the top step. It was though she (obviously a hungry mother with two or three babies somewhere) wanted to say: "I'm ever so hungry. May I have supper now?" I got the food out of the trash can we keep in the garage. She actually waited by her feeding station for me to sprinkle the food on the plastic sheet we put down. Spoiling them? Probably so. But we did this in Massachusetts, too.

One time we were having dinner on our porch with a couple we got together with. There were more than a few raccoons down by the retaining wall, with young ones, eating away. And

Don, who had not witnessed this before, asked my husband, "And do you put out nice white napkins, too?" He was amused no doubt. But loving wildlife, we couldn't let these dear creatures go hungry. After all, they were here long before houses took over their habitat, was then and still is our thought on the matter.

Angels Among Us

This is what I call those people who go out of their way to show love for helpless animals, animals who can't say, "I'm hungry. I'm scared. Help me, please!" Angels these folks truly are.

I can't think of a more shining example of this than our close friend, Joan. It's hard to think of some species of animal she hasn't assisted over the years: dogs, cats, birds, horses, goats, chickens, raccoons, skunks, rabbits, possums, chipmunks. It would take a book to describe all she has done for innocent little (and big) creatures. And the colorful, delightful stories associated with them.

Someone dumped an eight-week old Rottweiler puppy into an industial refuse bin. A neighbor who worked there had taken trash out at the end of the day and saw the dog. He told Joan about it. She took this puppy right in and had her for eight wonderful years.

She volunteered one time at an animal shelter and someone brought in the cutest little dog. That particular shelter put a tag on animals that came in, saying 3 days left. This dog was at the end of the time. Joan was concerned thinking, what if they put this dog to sleep? So she told them call me, if no one wants to adopt this dog and I'll come get it.

A friend of Joan's from church passed on, leaving a dog no one else wanted to take care of. She took little Katy into her home and gave her unstinting love and care for over two years. If this was a woman of substantial means, it would be a different story. But she isn't. Yet she has willingly paid veterinary bills for animals, bills that were not always small. Paid them with no thought of what she could be buying for herself with that money.

If someone she knows had an emergency with an animal, and it was the middle of some cold, dark night, I do believe Joan would throw on her clothes, jump in her car, and be at their house as fast as possible. No questions asked. Just love, pure unselfish love for animals.

Then there's Susan. She works at our local post office. Has a heart big as a house when it comes to animals. At present, she has eight cats and four dogs. Every time I go in to mail something, I get an up-date on her charges. If a stray cat or dog comes anywhere near Susan and needs help, it is going to get it, more than likely. She did this in Florida for many years and has continued it in Tennessee. Her face positively glows with selfless love. How could it not? She told me once, "These animals eat better than I do." But she said it sweetly and doesn't begrudge them what they need one bit.

As with Joan, Susan's regard for animals doesn't stop at dogs and cats. There's Charles, a miniature, now famous pig. Gatlinburg is a town in the mountains that had a terrible fire some months ago. Many families lost their home. Charles' family escaped, but lost their house. Even their car was melted so ferocious was the fire. Charles managed to crawl into a ditch and survived, but was badly burned. He has made a full recovery with the help of vets at the University of Tennessee. They waived most of the bill and the donations that poured in were given to Charles' owner. But he refused to keep the money for themselves, and turned back what was left over for other animals' care. He's an artist, and put Charles' picture on tee shirts to sell for income. Susan bought one for each of us, and has kept up with the pig through social media, becoming friends with the owner. Just last week she showed me a video of Charles rolling in a mud puddle on their property where a new home is going up.

And a woman we were friends with when we lived in the Boston area was a paragon of helping helpless creatures. Shirley was a go-to person for local shelters for many years. Many was the time she would call us, almost pleading with us to take in some stray dog or cat. Her house was already full at the time. I regret to say we always turned her down. We traveled a lot then, and didn't want to leave a dog or cat alone so much of the time. However, we have tried to make up for it over the years. Remembering all Shirley did has inspired us to do what we can.

I've told you about 3 women. Of course, there are many men with hearts of gold, who are very generous in giving to animals in need. Whether woman or man who lives such a life, they are angels among us in my view.

We experienced, in a very small way, what these giving folks have felt over and over in their lives of showing love to God's creatures. When we adopted our little girl dog, it permeated our lives. Indescribably wonderful.

To give some background: there was this one day when my husband came home from the pet food store with tears in his eyes. "A pitiful little dog is at the adoption center, and desperately needs some love", he said. Not thinking about getting another dog since we already had one we had adopted a couple of years earlier, his words hung in the air. But not too long after, I decided to drive over to the store and at least take a look.

There the dog was, dirty, almost starved, shaking with fear--the light of hope nearly gone from her eyes. Her former owner or owners, they think, left her by the side of the road to die. Which she almost did. Not to mention, she had had no care whatsoever it was clear. I picked her up gently, cradled her in my lap, and began filling out adoption forms. This had to be done, as I couldn't walk out of that store having seen this little creature so in need of help. Did angels smile at this point? I can't help feeling they did.

The young man who helped me with the paper work asked with moist eyes, "May I carry her to your car?" He was so glad someone was taking her home as she probably had only a few days to live.

When I got her home this little trooper, so thin and weak she could barely stand up, actually climbed our back stairs to have a look at her new home. We gave her a careful cleaning at the laundry room sink, and put out a bit of food. I made a bed for her by my side of the bed just in case she needed soothing in the night. Several old blankets, a mattress cover, and a clean sheet did the job for what must have been the best night's sleep this girl had ever had.

The light that filled the room was intense. As I said, it was indescribably wonderful. This lasted for days. It must have been divine Love that was surrounding us all because of the purely unselfish thing we had done and were doing. Not once did we think, we'll get a pretty dog, one that doesn't need much care. The only thought was, there is this desperate animal that needs help and we had no choice but to bring her home.

The love that people have for creatures, big and small, must be unlike any other love one feels. How it's different, I'm not sure, and it can't be adequately described. It just has to be experienced. And people who are telling you about their dog or cat, or some other animal they love, can't put their feelings into words. But their faces say all that needs to be said on the subject. As anyone knows who helps animals, it's an experience that borders on the divine. Isn't selfless love grand!

Safe - Wherever We Are

Having traveled far and wide for many years, on business and for pleasure, I learned to take staying safe very seriously. It was important to my peace of mind and freedom of action that I understood what really constitutes individual safety.

What helped me immensely was turning to what for centuries people in dangerous situations have turned to. The Bible. There are the most reassuring promises of God's protecting care found therein. One of the most comforting and best-loved promises is the first verse of Psalm ninety-one: "He that dwelleth in the secret place of the most High shall abide under the shadow of the Almighty."

I derived from this psalm a feeling of comfort and safety. When we were first living in the Boston area, I felt called to go into a suburb nearby that was designated as not safe to be in. There was a lot of crime, and some unsavory characters living there. I was just getting under way in the religious counseling work, and I opened an office over there. My husband naturally did not want me to do this at all. But as he had already learned in our marriage, if I felt I must do a thing, I generally ended up doing it. All the time I took a bus into that supposed unsafe part of town, there was never even one unpleasant incident and I always felt God's protecting presence.

In these times of increased violence one needs to have more than just a comfortable feeling about his well-being; he needs to know beyond a doubt that he *can* be safe, whoever he happens to be. Driving along, going into a bank, using an ATM, shopping in the grocery store, staying home alone etc. And he can be, so long as he relies on the Bible's proven promises.

And speaking of losing fear of staying alone, my husband used to travel a great deal. We had no dogs then to act as a deterrent to intruders. Our next door neighbor worried about me. She asked, "Aren't you afraid of being in that house all alone?" I told her I wasn't afraid someone was going to break in at night. Leaning on what I had learned about God's love for us and His constant nearness, I lost whatever fear there was initially. Nothing untoward ever happened. I was safe all those years of John's traveling.

The five physical senses tell us that we are subject to material conditions surrounding us, even to other people who can be irresponsible, dangerous, on drugs perhaps. But from the Bible we learn that God, perfect Love, is the one infinite supreme power and that man is the beloved offspring of his Maker, never for a moment separated from God's all-encompassing care. And neither the victim nor the perpetrator of violent acts. This God-created man is the true selfhood of each of us. It has helped me to realize clearly what is true of God and man, despite appearances that would contradict that truth.

Christ Jesus proved God's care for man even when an angry mob led him to the top of a hill with the violent intent of throwing him off. We read in Luke, "But he passing through the midst of them went his way."

Jesus obviously fully realized the inseparability of man from God. He said, "He that sent me is with me: the Father hath not left me alone." Our Master knew that our real being eternally lives in harmony.

Because our true selfhood is inseparable from the almighty Father, there's a very profound sense in which we can say that safety isn't dependent upon where we are. Truly, our deepest need is to come to see more and more clearly our unity with God, with divine Life and Love--and then strive to conform our thoughts and deeds to the divine standard of integrity and goodness. God's child is never, for even a second, deprived of his Father's loving care, never out of "the secret place" of spiritual security.

Even if our job, or some other obligation, makes it necessary for us to go into a dangerous, crime-ridden part of a community, or if we live there, we can expect to be protected. We never have to give way to fear. As long as we abide through prayer in the consciousness of divine Love's presence, we will feel the constant presence of our heavenly Father, just as our great Master did.

And with God's help, we can be safe in all kinds of weather. The windows were rattling unnervingly that night during a nor'easter as they call them in the Boston area. The near-hurricane force winds were wildly whipping the towering trees surrounding our house. I was home alone, and I had never experienced wind so fierce. "What if a tree crashes on our house?" I thought. "I wish someone else were here." "What am I going to do?" This kind of thinking wasn't doing me (or anyone else in the neighborhood) much good, I soon realized. So I began praying in earnest.

For centuries, people who were afraid have turned to the Bible for God's help. And it was God who gave me the solid help I needed during the storm that night. These spiritually powerful words from Paul comforted me: "I am persuaded, that neither death, nor life, nor angels, nor principalities, nor powers, nor things present, nor things to come, nor height, nor depth, nor any other creature, shall be able to separate us from the love of God, which is in Christ Jesus our Lord" (Romans 8:38, 39).

I reasoned, "Well, if all *that* can't separate man from his Maker, then a fierce storm certainly can't." This description of "wind" from *Science and Health with Key to the Scriptures* by Mary Baker Eddy, also reassured me: "That which indicates the might of omnipotence and the movements of God's spiritual government, encompassing all things".

I loved the thought that God's government was surrounding us all--not just me and our house but the entire community. The fear vanished. I really *felt* God's presence, and it was wonderful. There was no damage whatever in our yard or our neighbor's yard except for a few dead branches that fell to the ground to be cleaned up later.

Newspapers and television weather channels give much attention to weather disturbances world-wide. They physical sense tell us that we're subject to the natural elements around us, and that despite the precautions we may take, we are still potential victims of damaging weather conditions. This may seem to be the case--and we certainly can't be blasé about potentially destructive storms. Still, there is no more reliable help than God. There is actually no other power.

Many passages throughout the Bible reveal God as the ever-present, tender guardian of all. And Jesus was certainly ever conscious of God's unfailing care for His children. Our Father never leaves us alone and unprotected. His comforting and powerful love is always at hand anytime we need His incomparable help.

In truth, we are not helpless victims of violence from weather. As the man of God's creating, each of us is governed by God, the divine Mind, the only real source of power and activity. When we realize this fact, with the conviction that comes of spiritual understanding, we can come through stormy conditions without fear or harm. "The history of Christianity furnishes sublime proofs of the supporting influence and protecting power bestowed on man by His heavenly Father, omnipotent Mind, who gives man faith and understanding whereby to defend himself, not only from temptation, but from bodily suffering" (*Science and Health*, p. 397).

Whatever weather threatens our well-being, we can meet it through an understanding of our oneness with God. A spiritual understanding of this is extremely practical, and it's accessible to anyone reading this book. You can begin right now to discern and put into practice these spiritual truths of God and man that will enable you to pass through storms with calmness and confidence that your safety under God's government is sure.

When we have to travel and the weather has turned bad, it's a time to rely on divine power to see us through. We need to place our hand in God's. One winter my husband and I were traveling to another state to spend Christmas with a relative. His aunt had recently lost her husband and wanted us to come to Austin. We spent the night in a motel on the way and woke to find ourselves in the midst of a severe ice and sleet storm. Other travelers at the motel said the forecast was so bad that they would not be attempting to proceed.

After carefully considering the situation and listening for God's direction, we felt it seemed right to be on our way. By late morning we were on the road. We knew that God would guide and protect us each and every mile.

During the day's travel we saw many trucks and cars on the side of the road with tow trucks working overtime to get them moving again. By the time we reached our relative's home after dark, we knew that God had shown us the way in complete safety. We could truthfully say with the words of a hymn, "Thy hand hath brought us/On through dangers oft unknown" (Christian Science Hymnal, No. 115)

Survival in WWII

When it's a matter of life or death, God's help can make all the difference. Paul, a very close friend of ours from Melbourne, Australia shared with us some of his harrowing experiences when he saw service in WWII in the Solomon Islands.

At one point, he was in a foxhole and what he said had to be God's leading, felt he must get out of that place at once. There was no immediate reason for doing this, but he obeyed divine direction. The very instant he was out, a Japanese shell exploded right where he would have been sitting.

Another time they were going across a raging stream in the jungle on a rope. The rope slipped down, and it looked as though he would drown for sure. But he was pulled to safety just in time. "It was a close run thing", he said. Paul told us that what saved him that day was something he tried to keep always in thought when he was fighting there in the jungle, something that had made an impression on him from his days in the Christian Science Sunday School. The teacher told them in one session that they were one with God, that God was with them in every circumstance they faced, no matter what they were doing or where they might be. God would keep them safe as they were His own loved child.

And Frank's wonderful proof of God's care. This boy, a very close friend of ours, survived fighting on Iwo Jima in WWII. It was such a privilege to know this former Marine who came through that fierce experience. Frank was just eighteen, still in Sunday School, when he nearly ran to the recruiting office to enlist in the Marines back in Oklahoma. This was Frank, eager to do all he could for his country. He was a friend of my mother's, a wonderful man my husband and I came to know well. We stayed in touch through the years. And several years ago, Frank moved only a few miles from us here in Farragut, Tennessee to Oak Ridge, Tennessee. It was a joy to see him from time to time.

He passed on only a few months ago, nearly ninety years of age. But I feel he's continuing on in his eternal journey with God. All of us who knew and admired him for his Christlike love he expressed to everyone couldn't help but marvel at his vigor and military posture. He seemed ageless.

Because of my close acquaintance with this former Marine and all the conversations we had about his unique experience and the notes I took, I feel certain he would be pleased that I'm including an account of this episode in his life in my latest book. He was always keen to talk about Iwo Jima and loaned me some of the books his fellow Marines had written about their experiences. I must admit, some made for grim reading for a woman.

And because of the interest in this particular conflict seems not to have diminished much, this first-hand experience will no doubt be something many of my readers around the world will enjoy. As will that of Paul Jones of Australia.

Enlisting

Frank enlisted in Oklahoma City, Oklahoma on April 7, 1944. He kept seeing the sign "Uncle Sam wants you!" He wanted to join the Marines because he had heard they were sent into combat very soon after training. Frank felt this was the best way to get into battle quickly to defeat the Japanese and help end the war.

Following is what Frank shared with me over the months we talked about his time in the Marines:

Boot Camp

I attended Boot Camp in San Diego, California for six weeks. In our discipline training we were told, "mine is not to ask the reason why, but mine is to obey or die." There was also fitness training, rifle and bayonet training at Camp Pendleton. I was qualified as an expert rifleman. We had island invasion simulation training, as well as gas attack training. I was assigned to 5th Marine

Division (out of 7 divisions) and "Spearhead"
Division after boot camp.

Travel to Training Camp

We traveled to training camp from San
Diego, California to Hilo, Hawaii. We traveled
on an APA (Attack Transport) 2511 miles which
took about a week and ran into rough weather on
the way. From Hilo we went to Kamuela, Hawaii
by train on flatcars about 3 - 4 miles away. We
went through jungle to a tent camp already in
place at Camp Tarawa. There were 3 men to a
tent. Kamuela was on a cattle ranch owned by
the King Family in Texas. It was a large area with
cactus. We Marines found you could eat cactus
berries. But if you did, you'd get stickers in your
tongues that would last for days. However, the
berries were delicious. This is where I met Ronald
Cunningham who rescued me from a tent of
"Yankees." We became close friends. Played cards,
taught each other sports--catch, basketball.

Training and Preparation

In this desert on Hawaii we underwent artillery training. We fired 75mm Pack Howitzers and practiced to prepare and shoot "cannon" on "piece" (Projectile wt. - 15 lbs) We took wire communication training/communication of personnel (CP). We learned to climb a pole and string wires for communication purposes between the artillery weapon and a forward observer.

There was also mental preparation with prayer and study in whatever religious beliefs we held.

Getting Ready to Go to Iwo Jima

For combat, we went back to Hilo, Hawaii, then on to Pearl Harbor 205 miles away. At Pearl Harbor we could see many ships in preparation for going into combat. We went near Midway Atoll (Island) on the way to Saipan. We went by Saipan -- US Commonwealth of Northern Mariana Islands. We traveled 3,711 on the APA. Got off the APA and onto an LST (Landing Ship Tank) to go to Iwo Jima.

Why Iwo Jima Was Chosen
For Invasion

I asked Frank this one day, and he said Iwo Jima was of strategic importance to the US because of its being only 650 miles south of Tokyo. Also, we needed the airfields for our distressed bombers to have a place to land. The island was 3.5 miles long and 1.5 wide at widest point (8.5 square miles). It was shaped like a pork chop and had an extinct volcano at the southern end called Mount Suribachi. This was 200 ft. high. (Officially the Mount is 556 ft. high, but that measurement is from the ocean floor.) It is almost the exact height of the Washington Monument.

American Preparation for Invasion

June 1944, 8 months before the landing on February 19, 1945, Iwo Jima was bombed by carriers and land-based planes from the Mariana Islands (near Saipan and Tinian). The Island was bombed 72 days before the Marines landed. In all, there were 5800 tons of bombs with 2700 flights by the 7th Air Force. 70,000 American assault troops got ready for invasion. There were 485 Navy ships involved in the invasion. Strafing had no effect! As someone put it, "The Japanese were not *on* the island, they were *in* it."

Memories of the Battle on Iwo Jima

We traveled by LST (Landing Ship Tank). The LST was designed to let tanks out onto the beach and amphibious vehicles "DUKW" or "ducks" (Detroit United Kirk Works) into the water. The Navy was shooting over our heads, swooshing through the sky. It was exciting. Doors opened on the front on the LST. The DUKW went down a ramp into the water. We landed on the 2nd day of battle, February 20, 1945, on a beach at the southeast base of Mount Suribachi.

DUKW Incident

These were driven by Navy men. The wind was high that morning. The waves were huge. Our DUKW started to go up the beach. The beach was made of deep, black, volcanic sand. The DUKW could not get enough traction. Wheels were spinning in the sand. The driver backed the DUKW into the water to make another attempt. But the waves were so large from the high winds that the DUKW turned parallel to the beach. Then the DUKW turned over in the water and dumped us out into the water. My friend and fellow Marine, Ronald Cunningham, who had been previously trained to drive a DUKW knew the driver should never let the vehicle get parallel with the beach because it could turn over, which it did. Before the DUKW turned over, Ronald got into front end and said to me loudly, "Frank, you better jump!" Ronald jumped off safely onto the edge of the beach. I stayed down inside the

DUKW for protection from being shot at by the Japanese. The next wave turned the DUKW over in the water and dumped those remaining out.

While I was in the water, a quote from *Science and Health* came to me. The quote is called the "Scientific Statement of Being" which declares in part: "There is no life, truth, intelligence, nor substance in matter. All is infinite Mind and its infinite manifestation…" I was not afraid because I had been thinking of God's protecting power. When I stood up, the water was up to about my chest. Ronald came down from the beach and reached out his hand to help get me out of the way of being hit by the DUKW. The DUKW weighed several thousand pounds, and thus Ronald saved my life that day. I was forever after grateful to Ron for his strong arm and grip to help save my life during the landing.

As we were on the beach, a Top Sergeant came up and told us to lay down in the trench until time to go up to the artillery weapons. Feeling lucky to be alive, I later wrote to Top Sergeant Arthur E. Sauter. He was still in the Marine

Corps at Camp Lejeune, North Carolina and had attained the rank of Captain. I asked him about his recollection of our landing. He told me in his letter, as the DUKW subsided with the wave, it again picked up and appeared to drop on top of me. I could have been crushed by at least 2-3 tons of weight. The next 3-4 waves caught the underneath side of the DUKW and turned it every way but loose. The Sergeant had made wise-cracks about all 3 men having to reserve a seat in church to thank God they were still alive.

The DUKW was flooded and finally washed up on the beach with all wheels mashed in toward the undersiding. Later, the entire battalion message center on the short was lost by one round of 260 mm Jap mortar, 9 men and 2 officers (Communications Officer and the Ordinance Officer). After 15 minutes, we crawled up to the weapons. They were located at the south end of the first airfield, near the base of Mount Suribachi. I had a foxhole to rest in right outside of my weapon.

What My Day Was Like

I slept in a fox hole with my uniform on and used my helmet as a pillow. You may wonder, how in the world could anyone sleep with that battle going on? My reply, you got so sleepy you couldn't help but fall asleep. It didn't matter where you were or what you were doing at the time.

We took turns firing the weapon which was a 75mm Pack Howitzer. I would load and fire the weapon. For me to fire the weapon, the 3-striped Sergeant, the man in charge of our artillery weapon with 5 men under him, had communication with the forward observer. They would say, move to left or right to elevate. They could set the timing on the projectile when to explode. If you didn't set it, it would explode on impact. On one occasion, I was told to Fire At Will, as fast as I could. Fire, reload, continue. I did for many rounds until the barrel started smoking. The Sergeant said to stop, then mopped the weapon out with water. We were on 4 hours, off 4 hours. Mortar fire dropped in and around us day and night. Each night, there would be a number of flares that we would shoot up into the sky. These flares had parachutes on them and floated down slowly and lit up the whole island. This allowed us to see the Japanese more clearly at night.

The Raising of That Flag

I observed the flag raising on Mount Suribachi on February 23, 1945, on my 4th day on Iwo Jima. A sight never to be forgotten, a sight that when I see it in documentaries on WWII feel such a thrill. And I was there nearby. When this happened, *everyone* was yelling, "Look at the flag!" I turned back and saw the flag from where I was, about 300 yards away. I could see it clearly. This was a tremendous morale booster. Also, the ships offshore were sounding their horns in celebration. They could tell we were winning the battle.

Pancakes on a Shovel

As to food, now and then we would have a power bar which tasted so good. Much like one of our granola bars I imagine. The Marine Sergeant knew we had been eating C-rations and K-rations. In order to give us something more pleasant to eat, he thought of cooking some pancakes on a shovel. The CB's (Construction Battalion) a.k.a. "Sea-Bees" were professional road builders and able to build things that were needed. They had access to good food. So the Sergeant went to the CB's and got ingredients for pancakes. They didn't have syrup, so we contributed marmalade from our rations. In the rations, we had tropical butter that wouldn't melt in the sun. So we had tropical butter with marmalade on pancakes. They tasted SO good.

Fighting Over

Fighting had stopped. We *thought* it was over. But our Sergeant was on one side of the sand bag emplacement and I on the other, when without warning a bullet came through the opening of the north end of the emplacement and hit a sand bag between us and exploded. The emplacement was a round place with sand bags all around, with camouflage cover on the top, and with an opening towards the north where the artillery pointed out. When the sand bag exploded, a fragment from the shell nicked the Sergeant just below his left eye. The Sergeant immediately went to a first-aid station and had it taken care of. He eventually received a Purple Heart for that wound.

Another Glorious Sight

When the battle of Iwo Jima finished about 2-3 days later, we could hear airplanes coming. They turned out to be the "Blue Angels Air Force." They flew over the middle part of northern Iwo Jima, then flew straight up in the air, twisted clockwise, rising to a great height (about 1 mile) with white smoke coming out of the back of each plane. There were 5 airplanes in that group, which flew in close formation, then left the island to return to their aircraft carrier. This flight exhibit was to show American victory in the battle for Iwo Jima. The flight was beautiful, spectacular and a joy to behold! A great celebration to witness! All on the island and nearby ships could observe the show.

At Last, a Shower

My last day on Iwo Jima was day 26. Total combat was 36 days and mine was 24 days. I was about 20 lbs. thinner when it was over. When the fighting stopped on that side of the island, we boarded a ship. When we got aboard the ship, they were loading a number of wounded Marines. It was a pathetic sight. They were severely injured. We were allowed to take a shower for the first time since we landed. We were allowed about 5 minutes in the shower because fresh water aboard the ship was limited. No one can imagine how good that shower felt!

Frank said in his book, "Marine Veteran Frank L. Pryor - WWII Remembrances (2009):

"I attribute the wonderful way in which I was protected in combat to God, to my study of and diligent devotion to the teachings of Christian Science and the prayerful work of relatives and friends."

And finally on the subject of his religious beliefs which he held all his life, Frank told me he took with him into basic training, the intensified training in Hawaii, and on the ship and into battle what is called the service editions of the Bible and *Science and Health*. They were very small and could be carried by the servicemen. The Christian Science Church in Boston furnished these special editions to servicemen. My husband, being in the Army, of course has a set. I also have these books which I keep in my car.

Even during those 3 weeks on the island of Iwo Jima when things were quieter, Frank told me he would read the daily Bible Lesson from his 2 books. It is remarkable what these men went through, and how they were able to have some semblance of normality nonetheless. And how wonderful it was that both friends of ours, Paul and Frank, were upheld by God's omnipotent hand.

My Garden Bench

I didn't want to leave Massachusetts. Loved its cultural amenities and beautiful scenery. But as it is with these things, something better, though different, was in store.

After years of living in New England, there were my favorite haunts in Nature, places to roam, sit out and contemplate the loveliness all around. It was the giant trees that had weathered so much I would miss the most. Friends they were.

One March 31st esteemed weathermen predicted a smattering of snow overnight, perhaps. We woke to almost 3 feet. And after shoveling snow on 2 acres for many years, I taking the very long driveway and my husband clearing the back so birds could eat, he had had it. He began exploring a more temperate region of the United States.

Florida was too hot. And having grown up in very hot Texas, it wasn't for me. So Tennessee was finally chosen. And do you know? We were set down in a lovely wooded area, a forest I've come to think of it. Towering trees visible from nearly every window of the house. And a very fine stone garden bench at the edge of the woods. I had nothing to judge by, but the lady who had lived there before seemed to spare no expense on decorating. She and her husband had expected to retire there. But he was transferred to the Pacific Northwest with a job offer he couldn't refuse.

And in our new place, the daffodils I didn't want to leave in New England were everywhere. Being the warm South, there were abundant daffodils and all kinds of flowers, more than I could imagine where snow had lain on the ground well into spring in the Boston suburbs.

Wonderful things have happened while sitting on my garden bench. My first poem in my very first published book was composed there:

Light of Heaven

Candy-pink roses blow in cool breeze,
Care-free birds dart in and out of hedges,
Someone mows his lawn in the distance.
Of all the May delights that confront me
As I sit here on stone garden bench,
It's setting-sun rays that get me most --
Light plays on trunks of trees,
Light glints off rusting wire fence
A farmer put up long before we moved in.
But there's a thought much higher
Than enchanting light of earth --
It's something Christ Jesus once said:
"I am the light of the world: he that
Followeth after me shall not walk in darkness,
But shall have the light of life."
        (John 8:12)
The beauty of this Light
Can never fade to black.
It's presence and its power
Followers of His can never lack.

And our first cat, Mischa came up to me and let me actually hold him, wild as he appeared to be. Sitting there one day, admiring the bright yellow and cream daffodils on either side of the bench, here came this Tuxedo cat. My husband had been brought up by a mother who loved birds but disliked cats. When this little fellow would come around to the food left out for strays, he would be shooed away. He kept coming back. Then one day as my husband was filling a bird feeder, Mischa happened to purr and brush against his leg. After a few times of this, John said, "He's not such a bad cat after all." I was so happy, hardly breathed. Are we going to finally get a cat, I thought. I had had a loved Persian cat growing up but didn't think cats were on our horizon. It was all smooth sailing from then on and he eventually became a much-loved member of our family.

Having lived and traveled widely in Southeast Asia, residing in the Northeast US for many years (not to mention being glad to get away from the South upon marriage), I have to take care to not disparage Southerners. It slips out sometimes, my rather snobbish attitude, though

I am by nature a kind person. I don't mean to compare things down here with the energetic, polished, intellectual atmosphere we loved about Boston.

Then there's New York City. Aptly called a city that never sleeps. While I never wanted to live there, visiting was another matter. Loved trips to sight-see, give talks occasionally, just take in the rush-rush of the place. One day Trish, a friend who worked with me in Boston in the editorial department of a major magazine suggested, "Why don't we do a day trip to New York City?" So we did. Took the train from Back Bay Station and arrived a couple of hours later at Penn Central Station. High on our agenda besides browsing in the enormous Barnes and Noble Booksellers establishment both being writers, was having lunch in the famed Russian Tea Room. Just thought this restaurant sounded exotic, from a whole different world. It lived up to its reputation. And we had to visit the prestigious New York City Public Library as well as getting to walk through and admire Grand Central Station. It was the locale of many movies we had seen, as were other sites in the city.

After a very full day, we took an evening train back to the Boston suburb where we lived. John picked us up and dropped Trish at her apartment.

Back to what we loved about living in Boston for 25 years was the subway. The only one we had encountered except for a trip to Japan when we lived in Seoul. We couldn't get enough of riding on the MBTA as it is called. We couldn't believe all the riders with noses in books. People actually read books up here, we exclaimed. Being in love with books, we were thrilled. And those bookstores in Harvard Square. People reading, standing up inside the store, outside at the cafes. When our jobs permitted, we would make a day of it over there. Never tired of doing this.

And being classical music lovers, we had season tickets for the concerts ot the Boston Symphony Orchestra and Tanglewood Music Festival in the summers.

And we often went to the Boston Museum of Fine Arts. John was far more knowledgeable about paintings than I, and gave me quite an education in art, what made a particular painting a masterpiece, some background on the artist, etc. Not that I was artistically inclined, except where the written word was involved. John would bring home gifts of Winston Churchill books, about the great man and by him. I treasure each one.

And lastly about Boston, a place I couldn't get enough of, is the world-class Boston Public Library. So many rewarding hours were spent there. I can never be thankful enough that such a rich resource was made available to me, especially in the rare book section. This library opened up new worlds to me and awakened a yearning--and a resolve--to have a book of mine on a library shelf somewhere in the world, someday.

Most people, when they've been given good things, want to give something back. Such was it with me, with free public libraries.

For years, these public institutions had been for me a source of enlightenment and uplift, especially the Boston Public Library. One day while doing some research in their magnificent

Reading Room, the yearning came still stronger,
I must have a book of mine on the shelf of some
library to help others as I have been helped. The
realization of this aspiration was a long way off at
that time. But it did happen.

Our Master said, "Give, and it shall be given
unto you; good measure, pressed down, and shaken
together, and running over…" (Luke 6:38) Christ
Jesus had it right, naturally, as with every single
thing He ever said. And as a testament to the
way this eternal truth can work in one's life, and
as an encouragement to others who want to bless
their fellow beings, below are the foreign locations
whose libraries have my various books in their
permanent collections. The following list shows
just how far-reaching one's giving can be, to date,
and in no particular order:

Liverpool, England

Pusan, Korea

Beijing, China

Riga, Latvia

Helsinki, Finland

Poznan, Poland

Sofia, Bulgaria

Georgetown, Guyana

Lisburn, Northern Ireland

Coimbra, Portugal

Ostrava, Czech Republic

Rome, Italy

Rose-hill Mauritius

Pilsen, Czech Republic

Dkaha, Bangaladesh

Penang, Malaysia

Brno, Czech Republic

Launceston, Tasmania

Roseau, Dominica

Exeter, England

Llubijana, Slovenia

Gurabo, Puerto Rico

Maribor, Slovenia

Wanniassa, Australia

Rota, Mariana Islands

Sheffield, England

Hannover, Germany

Quezon, the Philippines

Devon, England

Rio Pedras, Puerto Rico

Canberra, Australia

Kintillock, Scotland

Warsaw, Poland

Rio de Janeiro, Brazil

Buenos Aires, Argentina

Cymru, Wales

Ngasaki, ,Japan

Dorado, Puerto Rico

Aberystwyth, Wales

Faduz, Liechtenstein

Barcelona, Spain

Stourbridge, England

Cork City, Ireland

Falkirk, Scotland

Birmingham, England

Majuro, Marshall Islands

Gateshead, England

Verona, Italy

Chisinau, Moldova

Kirkcaldy, Scotland

Medellin, Columbia

San Jose, Costa Rica

The Hague, the Netherlands

Erskine, Scotland

San Juan, Puerto Rico

Macao, China

Port Adelaide, South Australia

Katowice, Poland

Ottawa, Canada

Noumea, New Caledonia

Nicosia, Cypress

Guadalajara, Mexico

Coatbridge, Scotland

Manchester, England

Ontario, Canada

Alexandria, Egypt

Lampeter, Wales

Stirling, Scotland

Dublin, Ireland

Inverclyde Scotland

Bucharest, Romania

Paisley, Scotland

Beirut, Lebanon

Budapest, Hungary

Valleta, ,Malta

Blackburn, Scotland

Panji, Goa

Aikenvale, Queensland

Thessalonika, Greece

Glasgow, Scotland

Yerevan, Armenia

Dunedin, New Zealand

Clackmanshire, Scotland

Sao Paulo, Brazil

Blagoevgrad, Bulgaria

Wellington, New Zealand

Reims, France

Luton, England

Hamilton, Scotland

Regina, Canada

Thimpu, ,Bhutan

Hamilton, New Zealand

Ballerup, Denmark

Rotterdam, the Netherlands

Tallin, Estonia

Colombo, Sri Lanka

Grenada, West Indies

Halifax, Nova Scotia

Geelong, Australia

Thunder Bay, Ontario, Canada

Melbourne, Australia

Wenjian, China

Vaughn, Ontario, Canada

Singapore

Lanarkshire, Scotland

Vienna, Austria

Livingston, Scotland

Swansea, Wales

Chennai, India

Selkirk, Scottish Borders

Galway, Ireland

Hangzhou, China

Dumferline, Scotland

Kiev, Ukraine

Limassol, Cypress

Malmo, Sweden

Abroath, Scotland

Ayr, Scotland

Llandysul, Wales

Belfast, Northern Ireland

Nara, Japan

Okinawa, Japan

Bangor, Northern Ireland

Manilla, the Philippines

Tauranga, New Zealand

Greater Sudbury, Ontario, Canada

Brassov, Romania

Vilnius, Lithuania

St. Andrews, Scotland

Hastings, New Zealand

Kobenhaven, Denmark

Minsk, Belarus

Moscow, Russia

Trieste, Italy

Swaziland, Africa

Prague, Czech Republic

St. Thomas, US Virgin Islands

Malawi, Africa

Victoria, the Seychelles

Tirana, Albania

Bearsden, Scotland

Floriana, Malta

Aberdeenshire, Scotland

Harrow, England

Leicester, England

Orkney Islands, Scotland

Lisbon, Portugal

Monkton, Scotland

Addis Ababa, Ethiopia

Newfoundland and Labrador, Canada

Edinburgh, Scotland

Dublane, Scotland

Paris, France

Newcastle, Australia

Fort Saskatchewan, Canada

Renfrew, Scotland

Zurich, Switzerland

Inverness, Scotland

Isle of Man

Lyon, France

Clydebank, Scotland

Ceredigion, Wales

Hagatna, Guam

Nanjing, China

East Kilbridge, Scotland

Kuala Lumpur, Malaysia

Shanghai, China

Santiago, Chile

Copenhagen, Denmark

Kilmarnock, Scotland

Tokyo, Japan

Radyr, Wales

Seoul, Korea

Rekyavik, Iceland

Cardiff, Wales

Aberdeen, Scotland

Hong Kong, China

Dumbarton, Scotland

Luxembourgh

Bogota, Columbia

Raratonga, Cook Islands

Islamabad, Pakistan

Tbilisi, Republic of Georgia

Brisbane, Australia

Windhoek, Namibia, Africa

Limerick, Ireland

Dundee, Scotland

Bridgetown, Barbados

Suva, Fiji Islands

Milan, Italy

Naples, Italy

Lautoka, Fiji Islands

Would I have published books if we had not moved from the Northeast to the South? There is little doubt in my mind that I never would have. Why is this? Because there were so many prize-winning authors in the Boston area, I felt rather intimidated by their accomplishments. There were just too many for me to even contemplate putting out a book of my own.

But back to Tennessee. When we told friends were headed down here, they couldn't believe it. "You're moving where?" they would exclaim. One would think we were going to the ends of the earth. Or to darkest Africa. People in the Northeast are somewhat superior in their attitudes toward the rest of the country, almost to the point of feeling that any place other than the New York City/Boston corridor is a cultural wasteland.

But you know what? To our great surprise,

we found that Tennessee is one nice place to be. There's the warmth and hospitality Southerners are noted for. When we first spoke to a real estate agent in Tennessee about finding us a house, the friendliness over the phone was quite striking to us. One did not encounter such in the Boston area, people there being more clipped in their speech, less open as a rule. And it's so much easier to get where one wants to go. The housing is so much more affordable than in the very high priced Northeast. Probably why so many Northerners are down here. And we never expected to see the amazing creativity of the people who live here. Such diverse talent! Behind every rock and tree, it almost seems, there is an artist of some kind--sculptor, photographer, painter, writer, poet, musician, craftsman--folks who are simply doing what they were born to do. Or those who get an idea and just go out and do it. As one man put it, no one ever told them they wouldn't.

I so admire that get-it-done state of mind I've witnessed over and over by the men and women who live here. And I would say to anyone who has a desire to do more in life, as I did, try something they've only dreamed of but don't think it will succeed, go for it. Whatever field of endeavor we're talking about. What can you lose? I would tell them. If it doesn't work out (it probably will, however), you've gone further than you thought you could. And that courageous, some would say daring, step may just open the way for something else that will make life worthwhile. Not only worth living for you, but a blessing to many others.

Aren't we all capable of so much more than we're doing? All it takes is just doing it. If that aspiration or idea stays on the shelf, not only are we the poorer for it. Think of all the people out there who may not be informed/uplifted/helped-- whatever. We don't ever want to get down the road of life and have to say, oh if only I had done such and such. It's so much sweeter to be able to say, I took a deep breath and did it!

November's Trees

Flaming autumn leaves adorning trees are a delight to me. But November's bare branches, or nearly bare, are equally as delightful. Not everyone feels this way, I realize. Such scenes denote sadness in them, the end of something nice. But November's trees have a special beauty of their own, I find.

Shapes of limbs that aren't visible in full autumn foliage or in high summer present sculptures, reaching into the winter sky in all directions. Only nature could fashion them so. One sees such dazzling sunrises and sunsets through their branches.

Our library park put up Christmas decorations this year. And several of my favorite giant trees had shiny icicles draped on them. They hung down very low, a magical sight. They sparkled in the breeze, they shone in the sunlight. They actually looked as though it was raining. I would clasp my hands in a child's joy at the sight.

Then there's winter trees in fog. Ghostly? Not to me. Limbs take on a mystical aspect, mystical in a good way.

Closer to home, in fact just across the driveway, stands a very tall tree I often gaze at. I would judge it to be over 100 feet tall. What kind of tree it is, no one can say. Perhaps the man who takes care of our trees and shrubs will know. I will ask Curtis when he comes again the fall to plant three pale pink camellia bushes along the front of our house.

It's April now. And this particular tree whose bare branches afford lovely views of the sky at sundown and sunrise, already shows a softening silhouette. By the end of this month, limbs will be all filled in with spring leaves. Not until next November again rolls around will I be able to sit at the desk in our bonus room (what they in the South call a spare room that many homes have), enjoying the moonlight coming through the huge windows. Soft light streams across our Russian blue cat who slumbers on a cat tree between desk and window. Would that I could freeze this moment forever.

112

The Peace Christ Gives Us

"Peace I leave with you", Christ Jesus said, "my peace I give unto you: not as the world giveth, give I unto you. Let not your heart be troubled, neither let it be afraid." The number of men and women in the world right now who would give almost anything they own to feel some of this peace in their lives must be in the hundreds of thousands, if not millions. Serenity, when we aren't experiencing it, can seem more important than food or drink. Fortunately, we're never actually in a situation where we can't gain it.

If you and I want to have the deep peace the Master promised us and so obviously felt himself, a logical way to begin would be to cultivate the same awareness Jesus had that God is all-powerful and constantly near.

A life with peace and equilibrium can

be gained when we take to heart the Scriptural promises of God's ever-present love for us. We can learn to trust in Him and actually *feel* His constant care. This is a very natural thing to do, actually. For, as the Bible tells us, we are God's offspring. Material appearance notwithstanding, He has made you and me spiritually in His own image and likeness, and He is never absent from His children.

God knows you and me not as buffeted material beings but as His spiritual reflection, in possession right now of His dominion and peace--the same peace that Jesus manifested and said was ours. Christ is always at hand to calm any turbulence we may be going through.

Everything our Saviour said and did is worthy of the most careful study. An incident recorded in the Gospel of Luke, which tells about the time Jesus and the disciples encountered a storm on the Sea of Galilee, offers great comfort. When his frightened followers woke him with "Master, master, we perish," not only were the wind and waves rebuked, his students received a rebuke as well. It's interesting to note that Jesus didn't ask them, "Why don't you have any faith?" but "Where is your faith?"

Whatever personal storm we may be in the middle of, Christ is in the "boat" with us. It is always wrong for a Christian to let himself or herself become agitated, alarmed, overwhelmed, by human conditions. Why? Because to do so is to show open disbelief in the God Christians profess to trust for their life and well-being.

A tranquil life doesn't mean a life without challenges. The teachings of Jesus make this clear. "In the world," he said, "ye shall have tribulation: but be of good cheer; I have overcome the world." Abiding peace of mind isn't found in spiritual stagnation. Would we really expect it to be?

Our Master not only "told it like it is"; he showed us the way to behave as we're praying and working through difficulties. He didn't float above the human scene unaffected by the animosity, fatigue, sorrow, and agony he faced; he experienced life deeply. Yet he never let trials turn him away from his Father and ours. Nor should we.

Sometimes it's not the earthshaking troubles that disturb our peace; it may be common everyday worry that keeps us stirred up. It's no wonder Jesus spoke against our being anxious or fearful about anything, because anxiety selfishly foster that which is anti-Christ and makes serenity impossible.

However, by adopting Jesus' attitude of always seeking God's will, of doing all to the Father's glory, we will find that there is less and less left in human consciousness that responds to "the prince of this world"--to doubt of God's omnipotence, to self-will and worry.

Existence free from anxiety is vastly more than lack of emotion. There are people who, to keep some measure of control over their experience, suppress joy, warmth, acts of kindness to their fellow travelers on life's road. But this isn't the way Jesus dealt with everyday living. And it has the tragic effect of depriving us and others of feeling the presence of divine Love, which would enhance our peace and well-being. This negative approach to life yields through our stricter attention to our Master's commend not to be anxious.

Abiding tranquility carries a price tag. Through consistent, heartfelt communing with God, we feel the peace of our unity with Him as His beloved child. And how long should we spend in this prayer? Until our self-filled, materially distracted thoughts begin to yield to peace, until we feel some measure of conviction that God-- the all-directing, supremely governing intelligence of man and the universe--is indeed in charge of everything that concerns us.

The measure of our mental equilibrium is the measure of Christ expressed in us. The more we think and act in accord with Jesus' words and works, the more our lives will be increasingly free from anxiety.

And still more wonderful, we can, through God's directing, help others find peace of mind. They may want to know, "How is it you always look so peaceful? How do you stand up to things the way you do?" And when people ask, we can tell them about the glorious peace that comes to us because we belong to Him.

Independent, and Loving It

We knew, even before my husband's tour of duty for the Army was over in Seoul, Korea that we weren't headed back to Oklahoma. Too much family there. As much as we loved them, we yearned to be independent, as free of well-meaning interference as we could be. And loving the culture and the highly literary atmosphere of Boston, Massachusetts, that was the city we chose. Some Army friends we knew in Korea had already located there and we had visited them. We knew at once this was the place for us.

I don't have to tell you that our family was not pleased with our decision. Not at all. But we were determined to strike out on our own, come what may. We knew it would be challenging, especially financially. But this was something we just had to do. Being our parents, they had plans of their own for us, and did not want to see them abandoned.

I don't know about you, but speaking for myself, being independent is the way to go in life. Just do not like people draped around my shoulders, as it were--wanting things to remain static, rooted in a musty past. After all, no one owns us, do they?

As some friends of Samuel Johnson once said when they came to him when he was dining, "Sir, we have a claim on you." Whereupon the great thinker and writer replied: "You MAY think that", and went right on doing what he wanted to, paying no attention to their wishes to hold him back.

"But isn't being as independent as you describe rather cold?" you may be thinking right now. No, it isn't. Not in my view. There is nothing like being together with loved ones, yet apart, I have found. Much like two trees growing close together, but not leaning on one another. Or controlling their growth. This is the way it is with the relationships I cherish.

If someone truly cares about us and our

well-being, wouldn't they be willing to leave us room to develop and become what we're meant to be? I think so.

And if they're not, it may be an indication that they're thinking more about themselves than us. Thinking from a selfish standpoint, not to put too fine a point on it. As with those friends of Samuel Johnson, they were probably thinking more about not losing his enriching companionship more than they were interested in whatever new ventures he had in mind.

In my view of the situation, autonomy and kindheartedness are in no way incompatible. Having the courage to express both (and it does take courage we have found) has disentangled us from alliances outgrown; removed us from places where we no longer needed to be, freed us from having to conform to what other people wanted for us. When it's time to move on, we need to move on.

Yes sir, to me there's nothing like having the right amount of personal freedom. Being independent enough to think for one's self, to make mistakes for one's self even, to live one's own life is priceless. Just can't imagine life any other way.

"Still", you may want to say to me, "isn't being as free as you say rather self-centered, selfish?" It isn't this way at all for my husband and me. And those friends whose companionship I enjoy. As to marriage, we might not have made it over all the bumps in the road of life that probably most couples encounter without this advice we got early on. You no doubt have your own ideas about this, but I feel an enduring relationship is comprised of something a wise friend told us. In her long years of helping people with their problems she said, it became clear to her that these two qualities are necessary if a relationship is to work out for both parties: unselfish regard for the other, and respect for them. And it doesn't matter if it involves husband and wife, or two college roommates.

Our married life has been full of unselfishness and self-sacrificing. One example that stands out was when I moved to Seoul where John was stationed. As I mentioned earlier, it was the first time I had been away from home for any distance and I was going to a place where little or no English would be spoken. Where I would be living on the "economy" as they put it. I was concerned about arriving in a foreign country and somehow finding my way to our apartment. It seemed very unlikely that John could get away from his post way up at the border of North Korea. But through much finagling with his commanding officers, he managed to be at the Seoul airport to meet me. He went way out of his way to do this for me. What relief and joy when I saw his face in the crowd.

There are many other instances of regard for each other's happiness. This one sums up for me the essence of a sound and lasting relationship. We had been married only for a year or two, had scarcely two dimes to rub together, were living with rented furniture in a tiny apartment in Aberdeen, Maryland where John was sent to begin his Army stint. But we were happy nonetheless. I had received my first check for some writing I had done. All of $15! I felt like Rockefeller. While I could have used this for something for myself, like clothes, I decided to spend it on what I knew John would like which we couldn't afford. A ritzy ice cream sundae.

We'd heard of a very nice ice cream parlor in Baltimore. It was some distance away, but I had money for extra gas. We picked out just the right quaint, wrought-iron table and chairs. This place was quite expensive, so we ordered one sundae. The waiter brought us two spoons and to this day I can still taste that ice cream, hot fudge topping, and whipped cream. And the fancy little cookies alongside. It was a magical time we shared that day. I'm sure if one of us had a last piece of bread, we'd want the other one to have it.

Of course, common interests and aspirations make for compatibility between two people. But in my book, caring unselfishly about one's partner in life and respecting them make for an enduring relationship. And giving the other the independence we want for ourselves.

Never Shut Down

The woman sitting down the bench from me that day told me she had just retired. "I don't know what to do all day. There's not enough to fill the hours", she lamented. An air of boredom, almost dejection, hovered over her. How very sad, I thought.

Although decades away from so-called retirement myself, something about this woman made the vow, "I'm never going to give up an active life". And I haven't.

With so much to learn and see and do in life, why shut ourselves down? As Arthur Fiedler, the long-time conductor of the Boston Pops Orchestra once said in an interview, "He who rests, rots." And Albert Schweitzer wrote: "The great secret of success is to go through life as a man who never gets used up." Both these pieces of advice from men who led very productive lives well into their later years have stayed with me.

After all, age is so mental, don't you think? I've known individuals who were quite young in years who already had an aspect about them of being out to pasture, so to speak. And conversely, those inspiring men and women who not only acted youthful, they looked that way. How could they not, given their lives of meaningful activity and usefulness to their communities. Often the whole world.

When it comes to the subject of retiring, one finds divided feelings of course. Some are for, some vehemently against. To one person, retirement conveys the picture of long-awaited leisure, to another the dread of enforced idleness, unhappiness, and loss of purpose.

But whether one's personal preference is for a rest or for continued activity, he could scarcely look forward to experiencing what one dictionary says about retire, which is, in part, to "retreat", "recede", or "withdraw".

My thought on this is that while withdrawing from certain human commitments does provide a welcome change in one's lifestyle, we don't have to leave behind a sense of purpose. Without this sense of having some contribution to make, can all the travel, excitement, social diversions, and hobbies in the world fill the void?

When the feeling of "What am I really living for?" overtakes one, this may be an indication that he is actually ready to think about helping others, doing some good in the world, forgetting about self so much. And goodness knows, the opportunities that lie down this road are vast, for a person who is mentally and physically able to be up and doing. There's no dearth of humanitarian work that desperately needs all the help it can get.

Then there are the things one can do just for fun. Or for self enrichment, to keep one connected to the world at large. Lately I've been learning Spanish, with no particular time limit. I just want to be able to converse with the ever-growing Spanish-speaking workers we interact with. For example, the hard-working young man who mows our lawn, and does other things around the yard. He came here from Guatemala and helps me with my Spanish. While driving along, I sometimes listen to tapes and find this broadens me mentally. And recently, in replying to a librarian from Colombia, South America, who was adding one of my books to their permanent collections, it was exciting to be able to email a thank-you in Spanish.

And whatever one's chronological age may be, why do we have to shut down our childlike wonder and enthusiasm for life? And joy? Just one instance of this. You don't have to be a kid again to do many things. Like love a teddy bear. Or two, in case. I'm serious.

While my husband and I had teddy bears as children, we happen to still have them. To go back a bit, we've had them since Christmas 1986 where they were bought in Boston, Massachusetts. They're Russian brown bears, perfectly beautiful, and they were shipped from Korea. Having lived there for a time, it was fun to think of our teddy bears coming from Seoul.

We decided to give them names --Feelix and Feelicia. A boy for John, and a girl for me. Where these names came from who knows? But in those years when we traveled so much and had no children, not even a dog or cat to cuddle, we latched onto our bears.

And in a way, they've been a comforting presence in the various homes we've lived in. In the upheaval and uncertainty that come to most families I imagine, these teddy bears have brought us solace. They sit side by side on a chest of drawers, and each time we squeeze them (yes, we do) out comes love--years of love. I realize that people look to different constants in their lives to feel a sense of the familiar and for us, it just happened to be these stuffed animals.

So in my humble opinion, whatever makes you feel like a kid again when you are not, go for it. Who's to say it's silly, that you've outgrown such and such? If it's an outlet for affection, embrace it the way a child would. With delight and joy.

We felt like a child again when we got

our first dog, Dylan. And a couple of years later, a sister for him, Sasha. People would tell us, having an animal will keep you young, especially taking care of a puppy. And I do believe there's something to this. Being responsible for a dog or cat, and loving them, will certainly keep us on the go with far less time to think of ourselves. It seems to make us feel and even look more youthful.

Why would this so often be the case? I think it's because of the unselfish, spontaneous love these dependent beings get from us. Or at least I hope they all do. Such affection, in my estimation, is an aspect, a reflection of that Love divine which their Creator has for all His creatures, great and small. A person just doesn't have that much time to think about growing old.

In addition to keeping one young, a friend once said to me that what got her up each day as she was going through a rough time in her life, was knowing that her dear little dog was counting on her. She had to get up to feed him and take him outside. "It was due to this animal that I didn't sink into depression and just shut down from living altogether", she told us.

And I can't help thinking, kept her more youthful as well.

Of course, it doesn't have to be a beloved animal that does this for us. Anything we really love to do, anything that fires us up and gets us up in the morning (or keeps us up late at night-- whatever) will do the job. Whether it's a job we love going to, a volunteer project of some kind, or some outlet for our creativity, knowing we're doing something of use to someone, or the world at large, gives us a glow that preoccupation with ourselves just can't give. And in a way, make us feel like a kid again.

Not Even Shakespeare

Most writers I suppose would like to think that their words will be, if not like those of Shakespeare, at least somewhat long-lasting. Of course, not even the words of this great poet of humanity, as someone called him, will be around forever. But there are words that will be, that will be with eternally.

These words are those of Christ Jesus who said his words would not pass away. And they have not. They are as timely and potent and life-giving today as when they were first spoken.

Recently we saw a documentary about Mahatma Gandhi when something the narrator said jumped out at me. Gandhi, he said, would tell his fellow Hindus, "Unless you study reverentially all the teachings of Jesus, your life will be incomplete."

So powerful are these teachings, I couldn't help thinking about the lives of those Indians who were transformed as something Jesus said took root in their thoughts. This was the case with Felix Mendelssohn, composer of sublime music. He happened to pick up a New Testament one day and was forever changed by a statement of Christ's. Although brought up as a Jew, Mendelssohn at once converted to Christianity.

The young man from Guatemala who mows our lawn had a life-changing experience because of Jesus' words. We learned of his wonderful experience one Christmas. Although having known him for several years, he told us something completely unexpected as we all sat at the dinner table. His wife had prepared special Mayan dishes and we were finished eating when he said, "You don't know this, but I'm not the man I once was" We weren't prepared for what he shared with us. When he first came to Tennessee, he was apparently quite a rowdy individual   He drank a lot. And went to bars, getting in fights. He was arrested several times in downtown Knoxville he told us.

Well, this one time in the jail, someone had left a Spanish New Testament. Leafing through it, he came upon something Jesus said that he couldn't stop thinking about. The words made such an impact on him, he changed completely that night, he said. Stopped drinking, got a job, vowed to live the kind of life he knew Jesus would want him to live. As I said, this was such a surprise to us as we didn't know a more reliable, hard working, honest, meek individual than he. Every bit of time he can take away from the yard work he needs in order to pay his rent, he gives to help others find Christ, he told us.

"If any man be in Christ, he is a new creature: old things are passed away; behold, all things are become new" certainly applies to our friend. Given the divine fire behind Jesus' words, there is no life they cannot transform.

My life would certainly be incomplete without God's Word. More than this, life would lack joy and peace, and a sense of divine power with which to overcome difficulties that arise. How have Jesus' words impacted my life for good, you may wonder? How have these heavenly sayings *not* had an influence for good.

I could fill a book with real-life examples, but let me give just this one. I was working at The Christian Science Monitor. My desk was right across from a woman who was a long-time employee in the newsroom. In fact, she was secretary to the Editor and wielded a lot of clout. For some reason, she took a dislike to me and over time, began to make my life miserable. Things became so bad, I dreaded going to work each day.

Finally, I reached out to a Christian Science Practitioner who was experienced in helping people with their problems. After my lengthy recital of the wrongs being done to me, I paused to hear her ask, "Do you really want to be free?" This was quite unexpected, but I said, "Of course I do." "Then you will have to love this lady", my friend said. "There is no other way." Shocked was a mild word to describe what I was feeling. "Didn't you hear what I said" I wanted to say. Anyone could see I was in the right, and it was my co-worker who needed to change.

However, after I hung up the phone, what this woman had said began to take hold. It was clear that if I wanted to be obedient to Christ's commands, and certainly I wanted to be free of the discordant office situation, I would have to tackle this the right way. To say that this seemed insurmountable was an understatement. And I recall one afternoon while waiting for a commuter train out to the suburbs, I was walking up and down that platform in tears, so hard did it seem to get over my resentment of this fellow worker. "I can't do this", I said to God. "Ask me to love anyone but her." Eventually, however, Christ got the victory, And by the time my co-worker retired, we were very good friends, someone I was going to miss a lot.

Am I suggesting that once we make Jesus' words the focus of our life, all challenges will suddenly cease. In no way. I would be remiss if what I've written leads someone to think otherwise. There will be sharp struggles. But our day-to-day experience becomes through Christ much more alive--happier, healthier, freer--the way our heavenly Father wants it to be. And in the situations that once would have defeated us, we now find ourselves having the mastery.

Satan's attacks on us take different forms. One of the worse I've had to overcome is discouragement. It has seemed to drop on me like a block of concrete. "Give up, it isn't worth it" can nearly overwhelm at times.

Awhile back a devoted Christian said to me, "Discouragement has had me down for the count, not sure I could get up and continue the fight." The carnal mind's attempts to shut down our work for Christ can leave many of us saying amen to this.

But you know what? God came to the aid of my friend, as He always does for you and me. And speaking personally, I have been brought out of opposition so intense it seemed I could not endure it another minute. And what caused this? The blessed plain-speaking of our Master. Jesus never promised His followers a picnic on sunny days with balmy breezes. We have only to consider words like these to know better:

"Blessed are ye when men shall revile you, and persecute you,
and shall say all manner of evil against you falsely, for my sake."

"If the world hate you, ye know that it hated me before it hated you."

"If ye were of the world, the world would love his own; but because ye are not of the world, but I
have chosen you out of the world, therefore the world hateth you."

"Remember the word that I said unto you, The servant is not greater
than his lord. If they have persecuted me, they will also persecute you."

So comforting, so bracing I always find these statements. And there is this which always lifts me up when I think about it. Those of us following in Jesus' footsteps have the joy of knowing that we're in holy company indeed. To think about all those men and women through the ages who have given their all to be true to Christ never fails to renew my resolve to press on.

Our Saviour met every attack of the carnal mind and came through to victory. And so will we, as we *live* the words He gave us.

Our Master spoke words that will be forever lasting.

"Heaven and earth shall pass away:
But my words shall not pass away."

Christ Jesus